RESILIENCY IN SCHOOLS

DR DHEERAJ MEHROTRA

Contents

Preface

Resiliency in Schools as a priority talks about building the students stronger to face and overcome any failure. It talks about how a student learns to handle hurdles. Building resilience in students begins in the classroom. It is the key to making young people more robust and more assertive. Strength means having the ability to overcome stressful, challenging and sometimes traumatic experiences in our lives. The book talks about similar gestures in action.

Happy Reading!

Dr Dheeraj Mehrotra

www.authordheerajmehrotra.com

CHAPTER ONE

THE BUILDING OF RESILIENCE: HOW & WHY?

The priority:

Friends,

Resiliency in Schools as a priority talks about building the students stronger to face and overcome any failure. It talks about how a student learns to handle hurdles. Building resilience in students begins in the classroom. It is the key to making young people more robust and more assertive. Strength means overcoming stressful, challenging, and sometimes traumatic experiences in our lives. We build the culture with the spectrum to target an individual who is recognised, confident and can face any challenge in life under any circumstances. This encapsulates the response to the following notion:

As we know, as educators, Building resilience is key to helping students develop the ability to overcome stressful and challenging experiences.

Following are the 500 obvious ways and reasons supporting the building of resilience:

To make better citizens and achievers in their life.

It allows them to learn and grow in all situations – two crucial skills for well-being and development.

Allows children to work with skills and strengths in life to overcome challenges.

Managing problems is a priority.

Being resilient gives them the ability to tackle this head-on, bounce back from any setbacks and have the best chance at succeeding. It allows them to learn and grow in all situations – two crucial skills for well-being and development.

To grow as a priority.

To become a good person by overcoming their problems.

Move forward in life, able to cope.

Students develop skills.

They can grow up with good willpower. They can do their work. Happily, they can be more confident.

Because students need to be emotionally healthy.

Being resilient gives them the ability to tackle this head-on, bounce back from any setbacks and have the best chance at succeeding. It allows them to learn and grow in all situations – two crucial skills for well-being and development.

Students will be able to face challenges in their life boldly.

It allows them to learn and grow in all situations.

It will help the students to face challenges.

Higher productivity by learning and growing in all situations

To develop and learn to understand better in all cases.

Achieve flexibility, self-confidence, and perseverance orientation.

We are developing the student's skills.

To become a strong individual and have a positive attitude towards life.

Being resilient gives them the ability to tackle this head-on, bounce back from any setbacks and have the best chance at succeeding. It allows them to learn and grow in all situations.

Students will be able to face challenges around them.

Create good volunteers for society.

Students can score better in their academics.

It's the need of the hour.. knowledge and talent can not make a significant change if one does not know the value of overcoming difficult situations.

Being resilient gives them the ability to tackle this head-on, bounce back from any setbacks and have the best chance at succeeding. It allows them to learn and grow in all situations – two crucial skills for well-being and development.

Students must accept everything positively. Build confident.

It allows them to learn and grow in all situations – two crucial skills for well-being and development.

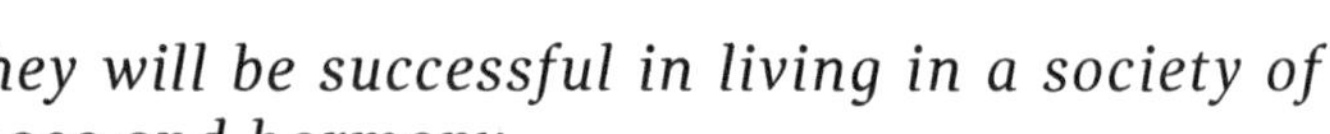

They will be successful in living in a society of peace and harmony.

It allows the students to learn and grow in all situations.

It will help children to handle the situation effectively.

The students must accept everything in a sportive way.

Allows the students to learn and grow in all situations.

Moving forward .... effective stress management.... increases self of belonging.

It will enable them to learn and grow incarnations – two skills that are crucial to well-being crucial skills for well-being and development.

To change their mindset.

Success in life.

Increases their confidence, attain their goals, and cope with depression.

Achieving resilience is very important in students' future. So the teacher's role is also vital during school days.

Being resilient gives them the ability to tackle this head-on and bounce back from setbacks. It allows them to learn and grow in all situations.

Being resilient is necessary to leading a happy and successful life.

For the whole round development of the students.

Students must learn to face failures and peer pressure.

Encourage students to develop positive skills.

Being resilient gives them the ability to tackle this head-on, bounce back from any setbacks and have the best chance at succeeding. It allows them to learn and grow in all situations.

Stress management and managing emotions increase the sense of belongingness, finding different choices, and developing of problem-solving skills.

Resilience will also help students approach new situations, people or experiences with confidence and a positive mindset, making them more likely to succeed.

It helps them to grow in all situations.

Increases sense of belongingness, learn to accept failure and develops problem-solving skill.

It allows us to learn and grow in all situations.

Development ability of students.

Develop a sense of belonging within the school community, and provide opportunities for goal setting and reflection.

Encourage goal setting; effective stress management increases a sense of belonging.

We are developing concentration.

Best relationship.

Stable and progressive individual, citizen, family, generation, school, society, nation.

Resilience is the ability to bounce back from adversity. It is a necessary skill for coping with life's inevitable obstacles and one of the key ingredients to success and learning to bounce back and bounce forward.

Some young people may face challenges with essential resiliency skills: physical illness, school change, transitioning from primary school to high school, and make-up changes.

Very important to teach this in this competitive world.

Students would be able to understand better and would be able to have good mental health and well-being and benefit from it.

Resilience is the skill that helps students to recover from failures. It allows students to learn and grow in all situations.

Development as a priority.

Make students mentally and physically healthy, develop coping skills, build confidence, set goals and become problem solvers.

A solid mindset to overcome difficulties.

Resilience allows the students to learn and grow in all situations.

It allows the students to learn and grow in all situations. It also helps them develop the skills crucial to well-being and development.

It gives people the strength needed to process and overcome hardship.

Teach students to become aware of when these feelings arise.

Resilience provides improved academics and learning achievements. Young people grow up to be responsible and committed community

members.

Success after overcoming the hurdles.

It allows them to learn and grow in all situations – two crucial skills for well-being and development.

It is essential to process and overcome hardship. If they learn it from this age, students can control their emotions better when they are adults; they can learn from failures and fight back to achieve success; it helps stress management. Overall grooming of students will be better if they develop resilience.

It enables us to develop mechanisms for protection against experiences that could be overwhelming and helps us to maintain balance in life during difficult or stressful periods.

It helps students to overcome stressful situations and experiences in their lives.

They understand how to face difficulties and become more efficient.

Being resilient gives them the ability to tackle this head-on, bounce back from any setbacks and have the best chance at succeeding. It allows them to learn and grow in all situations – two crucial skills for well-being and development.

We are making them successful in studies and their lives due to the generation of ideas of Resilience in their brain.

It is more critical for success.

Confidence and encouragement will only help them to overcome stress.

Community, society and all people help.

It makes them successful people by overcoming hurdles.

Being resilient gives them the ability to tackle this head-on, bounce back from any setbacks and have the best chance at succeeding. It allows them to learn and grow in all situations – two skills that are crucial to well-being crucial skills for well-being and development.

To cultivate a feeling of joy and Togetherness.

Being resilient gives them the ability to tackle this head-on, bounce back from any setbacks and have the best chance at succeeding. It allows them to learn and grow in all situations – two crucial skills for well-being and development.

Overcome fears and achieve success.

Learn how to cope healthily.

Set an audacious goal for students, look after yourself, seek help, and work towards a goal.

It helps to understand that mindset to be positive; every cloud has a silver lining.

It helps students instil in them a sense of well-being, how to overcome stress, effective stress management, increases their sense of belonging, encourages them to set goals, helps them feel at ease, problem-solving skills, and builds confidence that they can do anything, and how to overcome fear, teach them failure is the feedback only, cultivate feelings of joy & togetherness, learning to be relaxed.

It gives students the strength neededprocesssses and overcomes hardship.

Being resilient gives them the ability to tackle this head-on, bounce back from any setbacks and have the best chance at succeeding. It allows them to learn and grow in all situations – two crucial skills for well-being and development.

Resilience can give students the strength needed to overcome hardships in their lives.

Students need to achieve to reach their goals. We need to make them understand the 7 C's of resilience. This will make them realise their actual ability. To adapt themselves to work under any circumstance. Relaxing, setting goals, building confidence, positive motivation, communicating their problems and learning from failures are the essential aspects of achieving resilience for students.

Being resilient gives students the ability to bounce back from setbacks and have the best chance of succeeding. It allows them to learn and grow in all situations.

Health and well-being, encourage goal setting and develop problem-solving skills.

Give your student community a central platform to search for new groups and events, with one-click registration for any enticing opportunity. Being resilient gives them the ability to tackle this head-on, bounce back from any setbacks and have the best chance at succeeding. It allows them to learn and grow two crucial skills for well-being and development in all situations.

Resilience is an individual's capacity to cope with, adapt to, and recover from situations of adversity. This ability varies from person to person, is influenced by biological, social and environmental factors and can be taught and imbibed through the proper training and skill development.

Through teamwork and rapport building.

Students must keep going and overcome adversities for their betterment.

Helping students contribute inintegralal and interrelated components make up being resilient – competence, confidence, connection, character, contribution, coping and control.

To have better health and well-being, developobleproblem-solving, and overcome stress.

It can give students the strength needed to overcome hardships in their lives.

Imbibe 7c 's of resilience in students. It will make them better thinkers.

It allows them to learn and grow in all situations.

It gives them the ability to tackle this head-on, bounce back from setbacks and have the best chance of succeeding. It allows them to learn and grow in all situations.

To achieve their goals.

Developing is developing problem-solving in any challenging situation and cultivating the feeling of joy—the togetherness of pleasure of overcoming the hardship of life problems.

Make them more confident. They learn to face different situations and emotions.

Offering opportunities for students to sit without distraction helps them absorb content, remember it, and think about additional questions.

Resilience helped students develop self-confidence, learn from their mistakes, overcome stress, cultivate joy, and create a sense of belongingness.

Being resilient gives them the ability to tackle this head-on, bounce back from any setbacks and have the best chance at succeeding. It allows them to learn and grow in all situations – two crucial skills for well-being and development.

A student can cope with the fear and grow in all situations with this.

Being resilient gives them the ability to tackle this head-on, bounce back from any setbacks and have the best chance at succeeding. It allows them to learn and grow in all situations and have two crucial skills for well-being and development.

It will strengthen them and help them overcome any situation in life and be successful in every domain of life.

Learn to succeed by learning to fail.

Health and well-being,

It allows them to learn and grow in all situations.

Confidence is a choice.

Children will accept and adapt to situations and move forward. They will be able t manage stress.

It's a skill needed for students to deal with situations that are not favourable to them. Often they get anxious and out of control when facing difficult situations.

Bad times should be treated as a learning opportunity.

Can become confident, reduce pressures, and overcome challenges.

Being resilient gives them the ability to tackle this head-on, bounce back from any setbacks and have the best chance at succeeding. It allows them to learn and grow in all situations – two crucial skills for well-being and development.

Students can ve encouraged to set goals in their life. They can manage stress effectively.

Resilient Students sustain high levels of achievement, motivation and performance despite stressful events and conditions that place them at risk of doing poorly in school and ultimately dropping out of school.

Being resilient gives them the ability to tackle this head-on, bounce back from any setbacks and have the best chance at succeeding.

It helps them to cope with difficult situations in their life.

It will help the students to become good humans.

It makes them stress-free.

Resilience is important because it gives students the strength to overcome hardships in their lives.

Being resilient gives them the ability to tackle this head-on, bounce back from any setbacks and have the best chance at succeeding. It allows them to learn and grow in all situations – two crucial skills for well-being and development.

They will be confident, cope with stress, overcome hurdles in studies, set goals, have a positive attitude, etc.

It gives the people strength to process and overcome hardship.

It gives people the strength needed To overcome hardships.

It's essential as life is challenging nowadays. Resilience is important because it gives people the power .to process and overcomes adversity. Those lacking stability get easily overwhelmed and may turn to unhealthy coping mechanisms.

It gives people the power needed to process and overcome hardship.

Building learning readiness.

Proper development of skills and a smooth teaching-learning process.

Students can be stress-free, manage their studies properly, and achieve their goals by achieving resilience.

Resilience can give students the strength needed to overcome hardships in their lives. Stability will let students work with their skills and strengths in life to overcome challenges and effectively problem solve.

It allows them to learn and grow in all situations.

Students should get encouraged & motivated to do their work.

Being resilient gives students the ability to tackle head-on, bounce back from setbacks and have the best chance of succeeding. It allows them to learn and grow in all situations.

Being resilient gives them the ability to tackle this head-on, bounce back from any setbacks and have the best chance at succeeding. It allows them to learn and grow in all situations – two crucial skills for well-being and development.

They can learn benefits from copying skills, management and emotional control as a priority.

It allows them to learn and grow in all situations.

Because it gives people the strength needed to process and overcome difficulties.

The importance of achieving resilience for students.

It helps students to learn and benefit.

Encourage goal setting.

Develop problem-solving skills.

Learn to succeed by learning to fail.

Stability allows the students to learn and grow in all situations.

Love each other.

Students need to understand the stress and build an attitude of never giving up.

Being resilient gives them the ability to tackle this head-on, bounce back from any setbacks and have the best chance at succeeding. It allows them to learn and grow in all situations – two crucial skills for well-being and development.

Resilient students sustain high levels of achievement, motivation and performance despite stressful events and conditions that place them at risk of doing poorly in school.

Help to understand students' behaviour.

Readiness in the classroom, cand ultivarelationshipsship should help them to overcome difficulties.

It allows students to learn and grow in all situations.

The class will be exciting, and students will achieve their goals quickly.

It helps you take control of life.

Being resilient gives the students the ability to tackle head-on, bounce back from setbacks and have the best chance of succeeding. It allows them to learn and grow in all situations. They know to work together in a group.

Students can lead independent lives.

Give them the ability to tackle this head-on, bounce back from setbacks and have the best chance of succeeding.

It allows them to learn and grow in all situations.

To control stress coming into students' minds.

Encourage goal setting, develop problem-solving skills, develop problem-solving skills, learn to succeed by learning to fail, and cultivate a feeling of joy with togetherness at work.

It helps them to perform better in their work in future.

Being resilient gives them the ability to tackle this head-on, bounce back from any setbacks and have the best chance at succeeding. It allows them to learn and grow in all situations – two crucial skills for well-being and development.

It allows them to learn and grow in all situations – two crucial skills for well-being and development.

Being resilient gives them the ability to tackle this head-on, bounce back from any setbacks and have the best chance at succeeding. It allows them to learn and grow in all situations – two crucial skills for well-being and development.

Time management and relief from stress are a priority again.

Being resilient gives them the ability to tackle this head-on, bounce back from any setbacks and have the best chance at succeeding. It allows them to learn and grow in all situations – two crucial skills for well-being and development.

So that they will not deviate from their goal.

To be self-aware and self-confident.

It allows them to learn and grow in all situations.

It makes them ready to face challenges in future.

IT is essential for students.

Being resilient gives them the ability to tackle this head-on, bounce back from any setbacks and have the best chance at succeeding. It allows them to learn and grow in all situations – two crucial skills for well-being and development.

It provides children to cope with misunderstandings, control themselves and achieve their goals effectively.

They become more confident they can learn to manage failures. Ability to bounce back effectively and be lifelong learners, always ready to learn, unlearn and re-learn.

They will learn from their mistakes.

To practise thought awareness.

Learning to be relax

Set some goals to dwell confidence.

Being resilient gives them the ability to tackle this head-on, bounce back from any setbacks and have the best chance at succeeding. It allows them to learn and grow in all situations – two crucial skills for well-being and development.

Help in gaining knowledge.

To control any situation in life.

Silence can offer deeper and broader learning.

Helping other students contribute to cartouche city to help develop new skills.

Children will be confident and feel free to think of themselves properly.

It supports overcoming hardship.

They manage their situation according to their needs.

Helpful in life.

It's essential because it can help the student the strength needed to overcome hardship in their lives. It helps them to recover from difficulties and bounce back quickly.

A healthy body comes from a peaceful mind, so being positive, whatever comes and accepting, is the door to success; learning new things is always beneficial.

Give your student's community a central platform to search for new groups and events with one -click and registration for any enticing opportunities. Bei. Ng resilient gives them the ability to tackle this head-on, bounce back from setbacks and have the best chance of succeeding. It allows them to learn and grow two crucial skills for well-being and development in all situations.

It allows them to learn and grow in all situations.

To achieve their goals.

Encourage goal setting, self-care, and mindfulness.

Students do work hard. Activities.

To remove complexity.

It's essential to make understand students.

It helps the students bounce back from stressful situations, become more decisive and assertive, and succeed.

Adapting factors will be increased.

To encourage the student to focus and build on their strengths. When they handle a situation capably, acknowledge what they have done well.

For a better life.

Achieving resilience for students is essential for the following reasons -

- *To maintain a healthy life.*
- *To encourage goal setting.*
- *For effective stress management*
-

Benefitting from coping skills

- *For emotional regulation*
- *For reducing reduce perfectionist tendencies.*
- *For alleviating imposter syndrome*
- *To increase a sense of belonging.*

Students will be able to handle and overcome the problems that may come in their lives and studies and live prosperous lives.

.It allows them to learn and grow in all situations.

As it is essential to achieve the Goal.

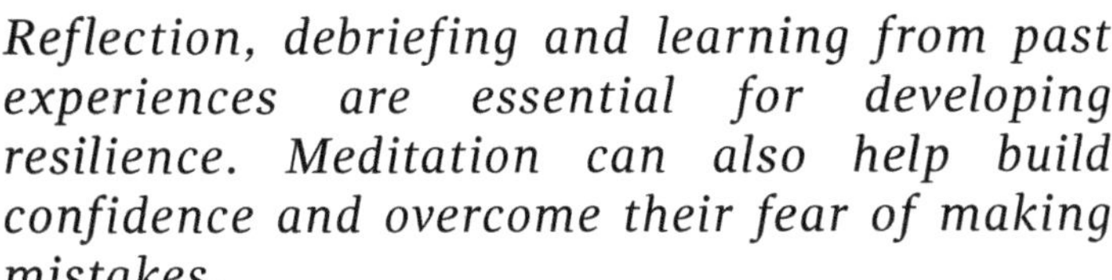

Reflection, debriefing and learning from past experiences are essential for developing resilience. Meditation can also help build confidence and overcome their fear of making mistakes.

Resilience is important because it gives people the strength to process and overcome hardship.

Uncertain the approach. Challenges to teachers. Some reflection on the idea.

It helps students navigate difficult situations and make adaptations that help them perform well.

Students can develop resilience by developing a sense of autonomy to become independent

and unique individuals. Freedom can only occur through taking responsibility, becoming accountable, and being free of dependence.

Allow them to learn and grow in all situations.

Learn from mistakes, make a positive mindset, and have positive relationships and a healthy work balance.

Being resilient gives them the ability to tackle this head-on, bounce back from any setbacks and have the best chance at succeeding. It allows them to learn and grow in all situations – two crucial skills for well-being and development.

It allows students to learn and grow in all situations.

It helps the students to reflect on, debrief, and learn from past experiences, which are essential for developing resilience. Reflection can also help students build confidence and overcome their fear of making mistakes. Seeking feedback also allows students to navigate difficult situations and make adaptations that help them perform well.

It helps them to face the situation boldly.

Resilience helps students learn and benefit from coping skills, stress management and emotional regulation. It contributes to a reduction in perfection tendencies, alleviates imposter syndrome and increases the sense of belonging while seeking help.

They will come out with flying colours.

It allows them to learn and grow two skills crucial to well-being and development in all situations.

It helps them to understand the significance of failure and keeps students self-motivated.

To make class attractive.

Students can do better.

Students will be able to cope with the many stressful and traumatic experiences.

Good learning at every opportunity.

Teachers should Promote positive emotions in the classrooms; als,o they can teach the importance of health and wellbeing.

It allows them to learn and grow in all situations.

Health care is more important than anything. So building resilience is essential to cope and overcome the weakness. Children should become mentally strong. Learning to be resilient will make the children capable of facing the uncertainties of life in a better way.

Being resilient gives them the ability to tackle this head-on, bounce back from any setbacks and have the best chance at succeeding. It allows them to learn and grow in all situations – two crucial skills for well-being and development.

Learn how to cope healthily.

Allow them to learn and grow in all situations.

Resilience can give students the strength to overcome hardships and challenges.

Resilience is often considered a characteristic of professionally successful people.

It allows them to learn and grow in all situations.

Students need to face upcoming challenges boldly in their life.

Promote positive emotions.

Teach the importance of health and wellbeing · Encourage goal setting.

Develop problem-solving skills.

Practice gratitude.

Being resilient gives them to tackle this head-on, bounce back from setbacks and have the best chance of succeeding. It allows them to learn and grow in all situations.

Being resilient gives them the ability to tackle this head-on, bounce back from any setbacks and have the best chance at succeeding. It allows them to learn and grow in all situations – two crucial skills for well-being and development.

Resilience means that a student can overcome obstacles in their way, even if they are difficult ones. Strength is developed over time and does not typically come naturally to us. Power must be learned through experience. Students often face hardships and changes throughout their adolescence and early years, and they need to know resilience to make it.

Those students that lack resilience may turn to unhealthy coping mechanisms like:

Negative self-talk, Aggression, Substance Abuse, Smoking. These unhealthy coping mechanisms will affect other areas of a student's life, but they will also have an effect they will also affect their mental and physical health.

Allow them to learn and grow in every situation.

It helps them approach the solution in any stressful or challenging situation. Allows them to grow in any case confidently and calmly.

Make their self-confidence.

Write and talk about the setback and Human Residence.

To face challenges in life and progress further.

Through resilience, Students can come out from stress and anxiety. They feel joy and togetherness at work.

Studeessentialto accepts the negation from any part of one's life or overcomessssss the stressful situations in life.

IN TODAY'S COMPETITIVE WORLD, THE STUDENTS NEED TO KNOW TO BE RESILIENT AS FAILURE IS A PART OF LIFE.

It's essential as it helps students to overcome their weaknesses.

I am getting success over hurdles.

Develop problem-solving skills. Failure is part of life and learning from mistakes. I am overcoming stress.

Think positively.

Being resilient gives them the ability to tackle this head-on, bounce back from any setbacks and have the best chance at succeeding. It allows them to learn and grow in all situations – two crucial skills for well-being and development.

Resilient students can benefit from coping skills and manage emotional and physical stress. It will also help reduce perfectionist tendencies and increase a sense of belonging.

By giving them relaxation and a platform to achieve participation.

Being resilient gives them the ability to tackle this head-on, bounce back from any setbacks and have the best chance at succeeding. It allows them to learn and grow in all situations.

We need to encourage them and help them develop the ability to overcome stress, self-care, understand, and deal with fellow students.

They can accept change easily.

It allows them to learn and grow in all situations.

It allows them to learn and grow in all situations.

Life throws us obstacles at every twist and turn, and learning to be resilient will help students learn how to cope healthily. Resilience can give students the strength needed to overcome hardships in their lives.

It will be helpful for the future of children to face any difficulties.

It allows them to learn and grow in all situations.

It will enable them to learn and grow in all cases.

To be able to handle everyday VUCA situations.

Archive goal.

Develop problem-solving skills.

Give your student community a central platform to search for new groups and events.

Allow them to learn and grow in all situations.

Students must be successful in their goals.

In their education. They make their life happy.

Self-aware, not afraid to ask for help and team care.

It allows them to learn and grow in all situations.

To become a good citizen.

It allows them to learn and grow in all situations- two skills crucial to wellbeing and development.

It helps to build self-confidence.

It allows them to learn and grow in all situations.

We can achieve our goals in our life.

They can become confident and booming in their life.

Help students to look beyond themselves and learnt from others' experiences also.

It allows them to learn and grow in all situations.

To bring them to the line.

Being resilient gives them the ability to tackle this head-on, bounce back from any setbacks

and have the best chance at succeeding. It allows them to learn and grow in all situations.

It develops the capacity to recover from difficulty and helps to manage anger.

Achieving resilience in students is very important because being resilient gives them the ability to tackle this head-on, bounce back from setbacks and have the best chance of succeeding. It allows them to learn and grow in all situations – two crucial skills for well-being and development. Resilience will also help them approach new problems, people or experiences with confidence and a positive mindset, making them more likely to succeed.

Being resilient gives them the ability to tackle this head-on, bounce back from any setbacks and have the best chance at succeeding. It allows them to learn and grow in all situations – two crucial skills for well-being and development.

To solve the problems of life.

Achieving resilience in students is very important because being resilient gives them the ability to tackle this head-on, bounce back from setbacks and have the best chance of succeeding. It allows them to learn and grow in all situations – two crucial skills for well-being and development. Resilience will also help them approach new problems, people or experiences with confidence and a positive mindset, making them more likely to succeed.

Students can learn to face any adverse conditions and build their confidence to overcome the problems in life.

Being resilient gives them the ability to tackle this head-on, bounce back from any setbacks and have the best chance at succeeding. It allows them to learn and grow in all situations

– two crucial skills for well-being and development.

It allows them to learn and grow in all situations.

To give a chance.

To be a perfect person in all aspects.

Being resilient gives them the ability to tackle this head-on, bounce back from setbacks, and have the best chance of succeeding.

It is essential to let them handle the pressure of performance, accept failure in a few attempts, and help them recover from adversity for anger management.

Resilience प्रणाली से छात्रों को अपनी पढ़ाई पूरी करने में मदद मिलेगी।

Students experience a tremendous amount of physical and mental growth daily. Between school, co-curricular activities, work, and social life, teens face many new experiences and challenges. Being resilient gives them the ability to tackle this head-on, bounce back from any setbacks and have the best chance at succeeding. It allows them to learn and grow in all situations – two crucial skills for well-being and development. Resilience will also help them approach new problems, people or experiences with confidence and a positive mindset, making them more likely to succeed.

Overcome fear and achieve success.

Better control and confidence.

They develop problem-solving skills, learn to succeed (by learning to fail the first attempt in learning), and manage to control their emotions.

It allows them to learn and grow in all situations.

Stress management for the students.

It helps in growing and learning in all situations.

Children should develop a never give up attitude.

It's a pivotal factor to achieve their goals.

It allows students to learn and grow in all situations.

They can handle difficult situations appropriately.

It develops confidence, relaxation and success for the students.

To come out of problems quickly.

It is necessary for a practical classroom.

Resilient students sustain high levels of achievement, motivation and performance despite stressful events and conditions that place them at risk of doing poorly in school and ultimately dropping out of school. So the role of the reason may be central to educational resilience.

Resilience helps the students to learn and grow in all crucial situations.

It's very, very important to achieve their goals.

It allows us to learn and grow in all situations.

It helps them to learn and grow in all situations.

For their personality development.

For their personal growth.

It allows them to learn and grow in all situations and tackle and bounce back from difficulties.

To be resilient creates a great cult, and one can achieve anything by achieving it.

Achieving resilience for students is very beneficial.

It enables them to tackle setbacks head-on and assists them in bouncing back from any setbacks.

It allows them to learn and grow in all situations, just like an evergreen tree.

It helps them to learn and grow in all types of situations. And it also helps them to face their problems with various problem-solving skills.

By achieving resilience, students can develop confidence and control. Through this, they can overcome their weakness.

It allows them to learn and grow in all situations.

Being resilient gives them the ability to tackle this head-on, bounce back from any setbacks and have the best chance at succeeding. It allows them to learn and grow in all situations – two crucial skills for well-being and development.

Students learn tolerance and become confident.

We are focusing on the study.

To develop a better society, togetherness.

Better equipped to handle different situations and different people, Better human beings.

It develops self-confidence in students.

Because it gives strength and is needed to process and overcome hardships.

To achieve the goal.

Students can develop resilience by developing a sense of autonomy to become independent and unique individuals. Freedom can only occur through taking responsibility, becoming accountable, and being free of dependence.

Being resilient, the student gathers tips to understand things positively.

Students can perform in their best way in any situation by achieving resilience.

Thought awareness, learning from mistakes, and assertiveness will be with them, which will help them overcome various learning obstacles.

Resilience gives them the ability to tackle this head-on, bounce back from setbacks and have the best chance of succeeding. It allows them to learn and grow in all situations – two crucial skills for well-being and development.

It enables the students to learn and grow in all situations.

They are achieving their goal efficiently.

Resilience is important because it gives people the strength to process and overcome hardship.

Being resilient gives them the ability to tackle this head-on, bounce back from any setbacks and have the best chance at succeeding. It allows them to learn and grow in all situations – two crucial skills for well-being and development.

They are developing skills.

Understand the feeling of togetherness and joy of sharing.

It helps in effective stress management and regulation.

It will help our future.

Students experience a tremendous amount of physical and mental growth daily. Between school, co-curricular activities, work, and social life, teens face many new experiences and challenges. Being resilient gives them the ability to tackle this head-on, bounce back from any setbacks and have the best chance at succeeding. It allows them to learn and grow in all situations – two crucial skills for well-being and development. Resilience will also help them approach new problems, people or experiences with confidence and a positive mindset, making them more likely to succeed.

It gives the strength needed to process and overcome hardship.

Overall betterment and personality development.

Students can develop resilience by developing a sense of autonomy to become independent and unique individuals.

It helps students in their mental health.

Students can overcome hurdles and problems in their studies and life.

It allows them to learn and grow in all situations.

Good for students.

Being resilient gives them the ability to tackle this head-on, bounce back from any setbacks and have the best chance at succeeding. It allows them to learn and grow in all situations – two crucial skills for well-being and development.

In other words, resilient students sustain high levels of achievement, motivation and performance despite stressful events and conditions that place them at risk of doing poorly in school and ultimately dropping out. So the role of the reason may be central to educational resilience.

By allowing development as a priority.

Improves teacher ability and minimises teacher stress and efficacy.

Students will become stronger according to the situation and time.

They become Better humans.

It helps them to learn different activities in different situations.

It helps them retry the activities or assignments they have failed once but can succeed.

It builds up their confidence to achieve any goal.

Allows them to learn and grow in all situations. It helps them achieve a new position with a positive mindset.

It will enable them to learn and grow in all following cases.

1. Create safe and supportive learning environments.

2. Celebrate student progress, not just success.

3. Provide opportunities for goal setting and reflection.

4. Develop a sense of belonging within the school community.

They can face any adverse situation without being affected so much.

Teach problem-solving.

To build hardship.

Mind relaxing.

It allows them to learn and grow in all situations – two crucial skills for well-being and development.

Students will learn from their mistakes, develop problem-solving skills, be able to face life situations positively and become an asset to society and our country.

For teaching life skills.

It allows them to learn and grow in all situations – two crucial skills for well-being and development.

Students will be independent and good decision-makers.

Confidence and competition.

It allows the students to learn and grow in all situations. Celebrate student progress, not just success.

It allows them to learn and grow in all situations.

It is the key to making young people more robust and assertive; it is essential because it gives people the strength to process and overcome hardship. Those lacking resilience get easily overwhelmed and may turn to unhealthy coping mechanisms. Resilient people tap into their strengths and support systems to overcome challenges and work through problems.

It allows them to learn and grow in all situations.

We are making the students more robust and more assertive.

They can get achievements very well if they know their resilience.

Being resilient gives the ability to tackle this head-on and bounce back from setbacks.

For students, it is essential for their life because they develop their problem-solving ability; they can control the situation and solve difficulties.

Resilience is important because it gives people the strength to process and overcome hardship. Those lacking stability get easily overwhelmed and may turn to unhealthy coping mechanisms. Resilient people tap into their strengths and

support systems to overcome challenges and work through problems.

To bring back their confidence.

Being resilient gives them the ability to tackle head-on, bounce back from any setbacks, and have the best chance of succeeding.

It gives the strength needed to process.

They will be able to face the world.

The learning community play a crucial role in developing the skills which underpin resilience through formal and informal learning opportunities.

Life throws us obstacles at every twist and turn,s and learning to be resilient through it all will help.

Achieving resilience for students is very important because They should face all problems in future.

To stay determined and succeed.

Students will be able to develop willpower, confidence and determination.

It will help them to learn and grow in all situations.

It allows them to learn and grow in all cases.

It allows them to learn and grow in all situations – two crucial skills for well-being and development.

It helps children to learn in a healthy, stress-free environment. It allows them to set goals for themselves.

It helps them to learn and grow in all situations.

It helps them to learn and grow and accept changes.

Give them the ability to tackle their problems and allows them to learn and grow in every situation.

It allows them to learn and grow in all situations.

Allow them to learn and grow.

It is essential for students because all seven c's always have in students to make the extra effort and give more potential in their studies.

Being resilient gives them the ability to tackle this head-on, bounce back from setbacks, and have the best chance of succeeding. It allows them to learn and grow in all situations.

Resilience is essential for academic success; they will gain the mental strength to overcome challenges and hurdles and come out of difficult situations.

It gives the strength needed to overcome hardship in their lives.

Resilience can give students the strength needed to overcome hardships in their lives and come out as winners in all situations.

Overcome their weaknesses and encourage them to attend to their goals.

It allows them to learn and grow in all situations.

Being resilient gives them the ability to tackle this head-on, bounce back from any setbacks and have the best chance at succeeding. It allows them to learn and grow in all situations.

It allows the students to learn and grow in all situations. It gives them the ability to be self-confident, swims the waves, and know how to handle hurdles.

It allows them to learn and grow in all situations.

Many students, especially adolescents, can have difficulties overcoming their hardships. It is essential to give the students the strength to overcome these hardships so that we, as mentors, can teach them how to face any problems in their future.

It allows them to learn and grow in all situations.

Help them to learn and grow.

Being resilient, students can solve any difficulty within time and learn and grow in all situations, which helps them in their well-being and development process.

It allows them to learn and grow in all situations.

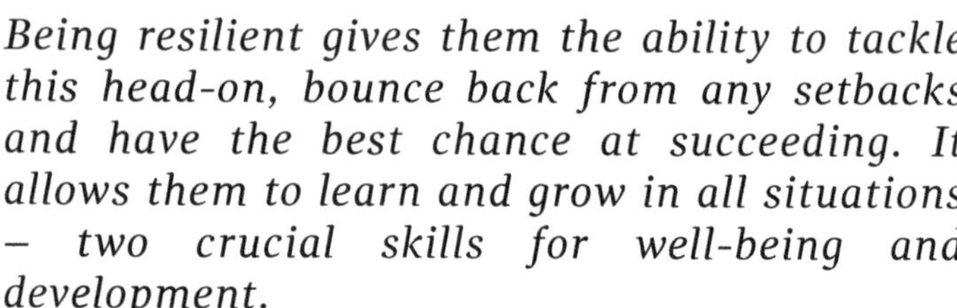

Being resilient gives them the ability to tackle this head-on, bounce back from any setbacks and have the best chance at succeeding. It allows them to learn and grow in all situations – two crucial skills for well-being and development.

It's essential because resilience helps students improve performance and achievement even when the situation is stressful. Also, it allows them to grow in every kind of condition.

It gives strength to overcome hardships, weaknesses, challenges, and problems at work.

And convert weakness into strength.

The process and outcome of adapting to complex or challenging life experiences, primarily through mental, emotional and adjustment to external. Focus on physical well-being, Practice relaxation techniques.

It helps in effective stress management and regulations.

Building resilience in students begins in the classroom itself. It is the key to making young people more robust and active and learning to handle hurdles.

Self-confidence as a priority has to be enriched within classrooms.

Achieving a goal should be a priority.

Being resilient gives them the ability to tackle this head-on, bounce back from any setbacks and have the best chance at succeeding. It allows them to learn and grow in all situations – two crucial skills for well-being and development.

Solid and robust knowledge about the taught topic.

Students can face situations, develop confidence, and develop a sense of commitment.

Effectiveness towards connection and solace.

Being resilient gives them the ability to tackle this head-on, bounce back from any setbacks and have the best chance at succeeding. It

allows them to learn and grow in all situations – two crucial skills for well-being and development.

They can learn and grow in all situations.

It helps students develop new skills, instil a sense of purpose, and learn and benefit from practical coping skills active, stress management and emotional regulation tools.

By resilience, the students can bounce back from any setback.

Being resilient gives them the ability to tackle this head-on, bounce back from any setbacks and have the best chance at succeeding. It allows them to learn and grow in all situations – two crucial skills for well-being and

development.

Resilience is an attractive trait with a positive outcome in totality.

Achieving resilience in students is very important because being resilient gives them the ability to tackle this head-on, bounce back from setbacks and have the best chance of succeeding. It allows them to learn and grow in all situations – two crucial skills for well-being and development. Resilience will also help them approach new problems, people or experiences with confidence and a positive mindset, making them more likely to succeed.

To overcome stress and have good health.

Settings are getting success over hurdles or difficult situations.

Set audacious goals and model learning from mistakes. Encourage responsible risks.

They can attain what they want to become.

It gives them the ability to tackle challenging situations, bounce back from any setbacks, and have the best chance of succeeding. It allows them to learn and grow in all cases.

Being resilient gives them the ability to tackle this head-on, bounce back from any setback,s and have the best chance of succeeding. It always allows them to learn and group in any situation.

Being resilient gives them the ability to tackle this head-on, bounce back from any setbacks and have the best chance at succeeding. It allows them to learn and grow in all situations – two crucial skills for well-being and development.

To teach students about the importance of health and well-being, encouraging students to find opportunities to volunteer.

It's too important for students.

By achieving resilience, students can overcome hurdles and become successful.

It allows them to learn and grow in all situations.

Being resilient gives them the ability to bounce back from setbacks and have the best chance of succeeding.

Training effectiveness measures the impact of training on the trainee's knowledge, skills, performance, and the company's ROI.

It allows them to learn and grow in all situations.

It helps students develop new skills, instil a sense of purpose, and learn and benefit from coping skills and effective stress management and emotional regulation tools.

Being resilient gives them the ability to tackle this head-on, bounce back from any setbacks and have the best chance at succeeding. It

allows them to learn and grow in all situations – two crucial skills for well-being and development.

Building resilience is key to helping students develop the ability to overcome stressful and challenging experiences.

Building resilience in students begins in the classroom. It is the key to making young people more robust and more assertive.

Training effectiveness measures the impact of training on the trainee's knowledge, skills, performance, and the company's ROI.

Resilience gives them the ability to tackle this head-on, bounce back from setbacks and have the best chance of succeeding. It allows them to

learn and grow in all situations.

Students experience a tremendous amount of physical and mental growth daily. Between school, co-curricular activities, work, and social life, teens face many new experiences and challenges. Being resilient gives them the ability to tackle this head-on, bounce back from any setbacks and have the best chance at succeeding. It allows them to learn and grow in all situations – two crucial skills for well-being and development. Resilience will also help them approach new problems, people or experiences with confidence and a positive mindset, making them more likely to succeed.

It helps students develop new skills, instil a sense of purpose, and learn and benefit from coping skills and effective stress management and emotional regulation tools.

Being resilient gives them the ability to tackle this head-on, bounce back from any setbacks and have the best chance at succeeding. It

allows them to learn and grow in all situations – two crucial skills for well-being and development.

It is essential for students to developStudents need to develop resilience because it will help them overcome academic difficulties and difficulties they face in their future lives.

Being resilient gives them the ability to tackle this head-on, bounce back from any setbacks and have the best chance at succeeding. It allows them to learn and grow in all situations – two crucial skills for well-being and development.

It allows them to learn and grow in all situations.

Because it gives people the strength needed to process and overcome hardship.

Being resilient gives them the ability to tackle this head-on, bounce back from any setbacks and have the best chance at succeeding. It allows them to learn and grow in all situations – two crucial skills for well-being and development.

Being resilient gives them Students will grow more.

Being resilient gives them the ability to recover from stress management and regulation.

Students can develop resilience by developing a sense of autonomy to become independent and unique individuals.

Building resilience in the students begins in the classroom itself. It is the key to making young people more robust and assertive and learning to handle hurdles.

Being resilient gives them solid feelings and being successful.

Being resilient gives them the ability to tackle this head-on, bounce back from any setbacks and have the best chance at succeeding. It allows them to learn and grow in all situations – two crucial skills for well-being and development.

Being resilient gives them the opportunity allows them to Always focus on studying.

Life throws us obstacles at every twist and turn, and learning to be resilient will help students learn how to cope healthily.

It helps students cope with life's obstacles healthily; it gives them the strength to overcome hardships in their life.

Resilience is the adaptability of students to cope with stress, adverse conditions and mindset.

Five ways to build resilience in students are promoting positive emotions, teaching the importance of health and well-being, encouraging goal setting, developing problem-solving skills, and practising gratitude.

We are achieving Resilience in Students to make students more robust and assertive.

Wellbeing and development to grow students with confidence and a positive mindset.

It helps in effective stress management and regulation.

Competence, confidence, connection, characters, contribution, coping, and control are prioritised via being resilient.

It helps in effective stress management and regulation.

Resilience is a fantastic skill that helps us recover quickly from difficulties.

Resilience is essential for students because this will help them overcome their academic difficulties and the difficulties in their future lives.

Ability to tackle any situation, bounce back from setbacks best chance of succeeding, and help grow.

Stress reduction.

Students should be trained to take constructive Management and regulation.

It helps in effective stress management and regulation.

It helps to manage stress effectively.

It's essential to achieve resilience for students. It allows them to learn and grow in all situations.

Students can develop resilience by developing a sense of autonomy to become independent and unique individuals.

About The Author

Dheeraj Mehrotra, MS, MPhil, PhD (Education Management) honoris causa., a white and a yellow belt in SIX SIGMA, a Certified NLP Business Diploma holder, is an Educational Innovator, Author, with expertise in Six Sigma In Education, Academic Audits, Neuro-Linguistic Programming (NLP), Total Quality Management In Education, an Experiential Educator, a CBSE Resource towards School Assessment (SQAA), CCE, JIT, Five S, and KAIZEN. He has authored over 40 books on Computer Science for ICSE/ ISC/ CBSE Students, over 60 books of academic interest for the field of education excellence, and Six Sigma. A former Principal at De Indian Public School, New Delhi, (INDIA) with an ample teaching experience of over Two Decades, he is a certified Trainer for Quality Circles/ TQM in Education and QCI Standards for School Accreditation/ Six Sigma in Education.

He has also been honoured with the President of India's National Teacher Award in the year 2006 and the Best Science Teacher State Award (By the Ministry of Science and Technology, State of UP), Innovation in Education for his inception of Six Sigma In Education by Education Watch, New Delhi and Education World- Best Teacher Award, BOLT Learner Teacher Award by Air India, 'Innovation in Education Award 2016' by Higher Education Forum (HEF), Gujarat Chapter, among others. He has developed over 150 FREE EDUCATIONAL MOBILE Apps for the Google Play Store exclusively for Teachers, Students, and Parents. This work has been recognised by the LIMCA BOOK OF RECORDS & INDIA BOOK OF RECORDS as the only Indian to draw that feast. Dr

Mehrotra is presently working as a PRINCIPAL at KUNWARS GLOBAL SCHOOL, Lucknow, in India. He has conducted over 1000 workshops globally on "Excellence In Education" integrated with Total Quality Management and Six Sigma, Technology Integration in Education (TIE), Developing towards being ROCKSTAR TEACHERS, including Cyberspace, Cyber Security, Classroom Management, School Leadership & Management, and Innovative teaching within classrooms via Mind Maps, NLP and Experiential Learning in Academics. He is an active TEDx speaker and can be viewed on the youtube TEDx channel.

As a premium UDEMY Instructor, he has also developed over 450 courses and is catering to over 8 Lakh students from 180 plus countries.

He can be visited at www.authordheerajmehrotra.com

Books By The Same Author

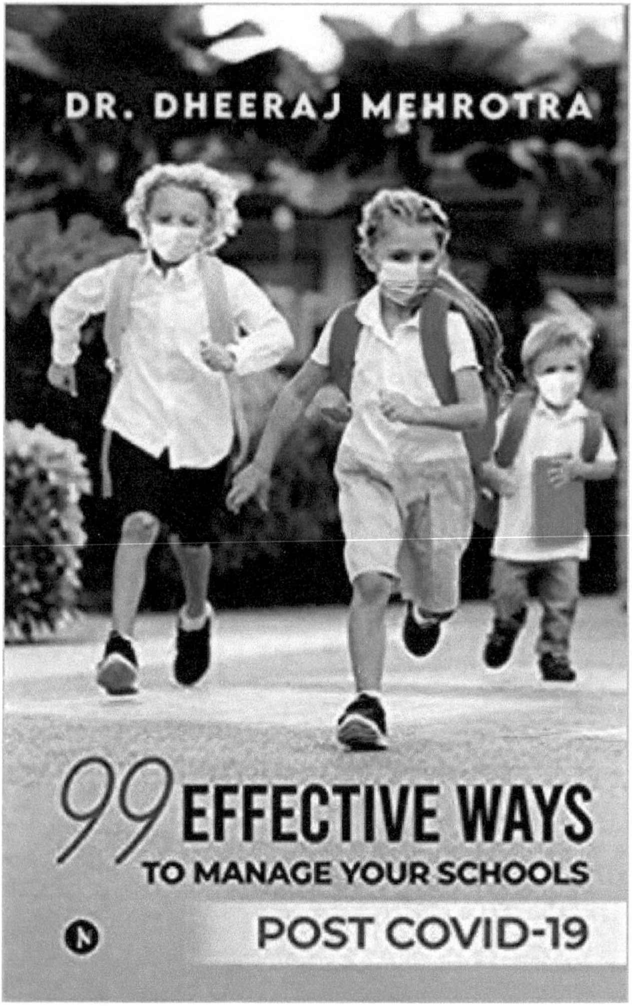

DR. DHEERAJ MEHROTRA

99 EFFECTIVE WAYS
TO MANAGE YOUR SCHOOLS
POST COVID-19

For Reference, visit: www.authordheerajmehrotra.com

BOOKS BY THE SAME AUTHOR

Printed by Libri Plureos GmbH in Hamburg, Germany